10 Ways to Write an EBook every 10 days

Shonda Miles

Table of Contents

To every writer who wants to write a book

You can do it!

Introduction

"The secret of good writing is to say an old thing in a new way or to say a new thing in an old way."-Richard Harding Davis

"Allow yourself to dream and fantasize about your ideal life; what it would look like, and what it would feel like. Then do something everyday to make it a reality!" Brian Tracy

If making more money, is one of your goals or if making money while you sleep is important to you then read on.

Do you want to write a book? Have you always wanted to write a book? Then now is the time. Don't put it off. Share your story with the world. Are you ready to write your book? Let's get started.

Brian Tracy says "No one is smarter than you and no one is better than you." This means if other people can write books so can you.

This eBook came about because I read at least 100 books on how to write a book. I would get motivated. I would start writing.

But I never finished any of the books I wrote. At one time, I had 5 or 6 eBooks almost done and 2 physical books that needed to be completed.

My goal is to have 100 eBooks on Amazon Kindle best seller list. My goal was to quit my full time job and pursue my dreams.

Based on my research, I knew I could earn $10,000 a month in passive income with 100 eBooks.

All I had to do was get these books done. I needed an easier way.

I wasn't lazy but I needed to get some of my books completed to build my momentum.

Based on my research, from each book I would earn $100 a month some more, some less, so I needed 100 books at least.

I loved writing so I could write and write and write.

While this doesn't sound like a lot of money, who doesn't want to make money while they sleep.

Who doesn't want to escape the rat race?

While I was doing other stuff, I knew this was a game changer for me.

Since I am a big goal setter, I set out to write 2 books a week, for the entire year.

I know this book is about *10 ways to write an eBook in 10 days* but I needed to push myself. I knew the only way to do this is:

    1) Set a specific goal

    2) Create an action plan.

So my goal is to write 100 books by December 31, 2016. I will write 2 books a week. I will measure this by word count and completed books.

Since I only wanted to write Monday thru Friday I decided I had to write 4,000 words a day or 4 articles-at 1,000 words each.

I also could record 2 hours of audio a day. Each hour of audio is approximately 10,000 typewritten words but more about this later. I love this because it is faster. Writing can be grueling every day, having that type of pressure on yourself.

I used the weekend to plan the next week. This included writing my outline and conducting any research needed. My goal is to write on subjects I am very familiar with.

Based on my research, on Amazon Kindle, it works better if you write your books in a series.

There is also strength in numbers. What I mean by this is some books will be instant hits while others will not. So don't stop at one book, write one after another after another.

Let's get Started

10 Ways to Write an Ebook every 10 days

1. Repurpose
2. PLR
3. Ezine Articles
4. Do a poll
5. Record an article a day for 10 days
6. Outline and record talking over the phone

7. Write a 1,000 word article every day for 10 days
8. Interview experts in your field or niche
9. Make a list of 10 to 12 questions and have someone interview you
10. Outsource the writing of your book
11. Wordbiotic

Chapter 1

"I believe that 80 percent of writing is actually thinking" -Tad Bartimus, author and journalist

Target Market

Who is your ideal reader?

Who is your target market?

Who are you writing to?

What problem are you solving?

Think of one person who is in your target market. Talk directly to that person.

Just in case you don't know what to write.

Make a list of all the topics you know anything about.

Positions you've held

Write down all positions you have held including parent and spouse.

Passion

Write down topics you love, hate or passionate about.

Interests

Write down all your hobbies. Write down topics that you know a lot about.

Strengths

Write down topics of things you are good at. Write it all down.

Write down everything you know enough about to talk 2 hours nonstop. Try to fill up an entire page. After you have done that next you want to take each topic or idea and put it at the top of a piece of page.

Then write down any subtopics/subheadings/stories/relevant quotes. You can come back and fill in any holes as you think about them. This works better if done in one sitting especially if you are a procrastinator.

If you get discouraged, close your eyes. Visualize yourself with your book on the best seller list on Amazon Kindle.

Do this several times a day. Repeat over and over. Say to yourself "I can do this." "I can do it."

Whenever you feel like procrastinating, tell yourself "Do it now." "Do it now." Picture the end result.

Whether you feel like it or not-get back to work. Get back to writing. Don't stop until you have met your word count for the day.

Don't let your feelings get in the way of you achieving your goal of being a bestselling author.

Chapter 2

Make writing a priority every day. Do it first thing in the morning. It will probably take you 45 minutes or less.

Talk about what you know.

Create a roadmap.

Write down your ideas when you get them.

You could easily write 3 or more books a month which would give you 36 eBooks on Amazon Kindle at the end of the year. At the end of the year, you could easily earn $4,000 or more in passive income.

The important thing here is to take action every day. Don't procrastinate. Don't wait until the evening to start working on your eBook.

Do it 1st thing in the morning when you are fresh and full of energy.

Work from an outline. It is important to write down all of your ideas on a topic. Do a brain dump.

Don't just start writing. Write down all your ideas on the topic. Write down everything you can think of regardless of whether it makes sense right now or not.

The next thing is organizing your list or creating a new list for what you might use in your 1steBook. Try to keep each list to about 8 – 10 topics.

After creating your new list for your 1ˢᵗeBook, you can start to write the step-by-step instructions, subtopics or subheadings to give you some direction when you write or record.

I find that if I make little notes on each article/chapter or subheading, when I get ready to write I don't forget my thought pattern of what I wrote down to begin with.

Cardinal Rule
Don't edit while you write.

At this point, I make a note of any quotes, examples or stories I want to include. About a year ago, I started to keep a file of quotes that I like. I also keep a file for examples that illustrate a point.

Read what you wrote out loud.

Keep a Journal
I keep a journal. I pull stories from it that illustrate a point for my readers. This is a good practice for all writers. Your journal will give you a ton of ideas to write about.

Think on Paper

Think on Paper. This helps me get clear on my thoughts and what I am trying to say. It is as though I know what I am saying in my head and but it not quite coming out like I planned for it to.

Then its Happy Writing or Happy Recording. You can organize your list into Chapters. Don't get bogged down in writing Chapter 1 just start with whatever chapter you want.

If you go the route of recording, you can use freeconferencecall.com. It really is free. You can record it anywhere.

You can have your eBook transcribed by Rev.com for about a $1 a minute. All you have to do is Upload your mp3 or mp4 file to Rev.com. They will have it ready in less than 24 hours usually. They will send it back as a Word or PDF document.

Believe in Yourself
Believe in Yourself. You can do this. If you only have 2 hours a week that is all you need to finish your two books. This does not include research and outlining, of course.

If you follow these steps you will be a published author for Amazon Kindle in no time.

Tips to help you stay full of content and ideas

- Read 1 hour a day on your topic.
- Listen to a podcast on your topic at least several times a week.
- Watch YouTube videos on your area of expertise.
- Listen to audio in your car on your topic.
- Read a book on Amazon Kindle at least weekly.
- Read a few articles on your topic at least weekly.
- Read stuff you've already wrote and it will give you more ideas.
- Read the blogs of thought leaders in your field.
- Keep a notebook and pen with you at all times to jot down notes or ideas.

Chapter 3

Use a book shell. If you use a book shell it will reduce the time it takes to put the same information in every book. Book shells contain the same information in every book you write.

Book Shell

Title Page

Copyright page

Acknowledgements

Dedication

Table of Contents

About the Author

Other Books by author

Free Offer

This will be the same for every book. What I did initially is open a Word Document and save it as Nonfiction Kindle Book Shell. You can name it whatever you choose. First Page I just put Title Page then your name underneath. This way when you write each book all you have to do is replace title with the Actual title but your name is already there.

You can have a standard copyright. It will be the same for all your books.

Copyright

Copyright © 2016 Your Name

You can just have a blank page with the Table of Contents on it. The About the Author is your Bio. This is usually the same for every book. Your books by the author will be the same for each book. Of course you will add to it as you write more books.

The key here is the Shell. You will start your book with approximately 1,000 words. This will save you a lot of time.

Each day you will work on a different way to write an ebook. At the end of the 10 days you will decide which way works best for you.

At the end of this book you will find a Quick Start Sheet for the method you like best. The key is don't give up. Try to write every day. Read every day. Capture every idea in a notebook or Journal.

Chapter 4

Repurpose

Do you have an article you previously wrote? Do you have old blog posts? Write 1 page a day. Write 1,000 words times 10 days. Have you written a book before? Have you written an eBook, report, any material you have wrote before now can be repurposed into new material? You can expand on points. You can rewrite portions of it. I have found if I reread a paragraph or even a sense I can explain things further or dig deeper.

Add a quote, story, action items, checklist and summary. After each sentence look at how you can add explanations.

PLR

"Another option is to use a site like AllPrivateLabelContent.com, which will allow you to buy the rights to content you can label as your own and you can revise it, change it up and sell it as you please. It's called PLR content or private label rights content and it's an option for to get your product together quickly."

Be sure you revise this and put into your own words. Add stories and your experience. This will bring it to life.

Chapter 5

Ezine articles

Take 20 articles from ezinearticles.com on your topic keeping the writers bio in place and publish that as an e-book. Aim for 6,000-10,000-word count. Make sure each article is a chapter. Of course you will have to read quite a few articles to get the best ones. You will have to organize the articles for flow. You can hire a VA (Virtual Assistant) on Fiverr.com to email the author of the articles and ask for permission to use the articles in a book. Most authors won't mind. After all they are getting exposure they might not have otherwise received.

You can create a Profile on Fiverr for free. It takes less than a minute. In the search box type Virtual Assistant. Choose High rating on tab in the middle of page. Select 5 and go to each of their page and click on the Contact me on the right and tell them what you need. It typically cost $5 maybe $10. I usually choose someone who will work for 3 hours for $5.

I would already have the articles saved to my computer in one file. You can do this as you read them and decide to use them. I would have the VA take the email from the bottom of the article with the Title of the article and send the email to the author. If the email is not listed, they can go to the author's website and click on the contact us page. Usually the email will be listed there as well.

I would have the VA send a short email something like

Dear The person's name,

I really enjoyed reading your article on ezinearticles.com. I am writing a book or compiling a book of expert articles. I am writing to ask for permission to use your article with the bio in place as is. If it is okay, you can reply to this email. If is not okay, will you please reply as well?

I would include your 30 second elevator speech so they know a little about you.

Thanks for your consideration.

Sincerely,

Your name

Your title

Your website

Your email

Your phone number in case they want to call you

Do a poll

Ask your customers what their problems are. Ask them what questions they have.

Write an article on each. Depending on the topic it could be longer.

Chapter 6

Record an article a day for 10 days

You could literally talk about a topic for 6 to 10 minutes a day and at the end of the week you would have a book.

Of course, you would have to have about 10 topics on which to speak on. This should be easy.

Read 5 articles on your topic and then write a 1,000-word article on key ideas. You can also read 3 books on Amazon Kindle and let the ideas flow.

You can also do this to write a chapter, you are stuck on. Whatever you do, don't give up.

Chapter 7

Outline and record

Outline and record it all in 1 hour. Instead of making a 10 minute recording each day, you can write your outline with your subtopics or subheading and record your entire eBook in one hour.

I can write 1,000 words per hour or I can record 10,000 words per hour.

Always outline your books. Always work from an outline.

This is an absolute must. Amazon puts you in front of millions it's your job to capture as many of them as possible and keep helping them if you don't nobody will.

If you want to build your list, then you should a free offer to get readers to go to your website and enter their email address. You can entice them by offering a free audio version, PDF of book, video recording of book, checklists, assignments, private Facebook Community. I've even seen people sell straight from the book. I've seen people seed their book with other books, free trial to membership, coaching, speaking.

The time will go by fast because you will be in the zone. Don't believe me, try it.

Once you start talking about an area you love you will find you can go on and on. This is why having an outline is so important. You don't want to ramble. You want to keep the recording focused.

All of this sounds good, but is it possible? Of course it is. What you have to think about is Why are you doing this?

Why do you want to write your first book on Amazon Kindle?

Why do you want to Self-Published? Why do you want to be an Author? Why is this important now?

"Without the why, the how would have been impossible." Robert Kiyosaki

Make a list of your Whys. Yes, write it down.

Keep asking yourself why - so you can really drill down why you really want this. This is an essential step to this process.

Nothing else matters. The truth is without the Why the chances of you failing and not getting your message out to the world is high.

Make finding out your Why your highest priority.

This rest will be much easier because of it. What does it feel like to be a Published author? How will you feel getting the checks from Amazon Kindle?

What will you do with the money? How will your life change as a result of achieving this goal?

What is the end goal? Why are you doing this? To write hundreds of books for Amazon Kindle. To become a millionaire. To build a platform. To get traffic to your website.

All of this is possible and more if you have a Big Enough Why. What is your Big Why? Is it more quality time with your family? More money. Take business to the next level. To do what you want when you want.

Chapter 8

Write a 1,000-word article every day for 10 days

Write a 1,000-word article each day for 10 days. You can write 1 article. The first one may take a little time. You will get faster and faster.

After you write it then go back and read it. Then reread it and after each sentence you can ask yourself what else, what else.

Just keep asking yourself what else might the customer need or want to know. How can you go deeper?

You will be surprised. Of course your article title will be a working title and you can have 2 or 3 subheadings if you would like to break up the content.

You can ask questions to make your target market think deeper on the topic. You want them to take action and change their lives.

You can add action items at the end of each article. You can also add a summary after each article which is really a chapter.

This will help reiterate or reemphasize key points in that chapter. This will also allow your customer to come back later and review key points quickly.

For each chapter or 1,000-word article you will have your content (the meat on the topic with quotes, examples or stories) to illustrate key points, action items and a brief summary of the key takeaways.

If you know your topic, you can do this fairly quickly. If it takes a little longer, don't worry just keep writing. You can do this. Keep the end goal in mind. You want to become a self-published author.

Amazon Kindle has made self-publishing so easy. You can have your eBook done in no time. All you need to do is make a commitment and take action every day. Don't let anything stand in your way.

The next technique is Interview experts in your field or niche.

Chapter 9

Interview experts in your field or niche

If you want to interview 10 experts on your niche, you can certainly do this.

In order to find these experts, you can go to expert.com, HARO, Google "podcast niche," Amazon Kindle, e-zine articles or Selfgrowth.com.

Look for their email or website. After you find them, then email each expert.

You can email each expert and ask for an interview. Make the email short and sweet. You could send a list of questions ahead of time if you would like (after they agree to the interview).

You can also ask the expert is there any questions they think you should ask them.

After you get the interview you can ask each expert a different question or a series of questions.

You can tell them you can interview them any time. People love talking about themselves. This will give them exposure to new people.

This will help build their platform. You can provide them with mp3 or mp4 if you record the interview via Skype, Go to Webinar or Zoom.

This is good as you can repurpose it. You can split up the questions into short YouTube videos. You can use this (interview) in a course or a membership site.

In order to streamline this, contact everyone by email, or via their contact page and ask for an interview. As soon as someone agrees to do the interview, try to get it recorded as soon as possible.

Be flexible. Don't waste time. You can start writing your eBook and continue to contact more experts until you get your 10. If someone declines, just move on.

Make a list of the questions you want to ask. Think about what your target market wants to know or needs to know.

I plan my interviews months in advance. I created a question bank of about 10 questions. I added to it every day until it was 25 questions.

Every week I would send out 10 requests for interviews or 2 a day. If you send out 2 a day it will take less than 15 minutes a day.

You can send the 10 requests a week, all at once if you would like. It should take less than an hour.

If you don't know what to ask, just ask them. You can do a survey through Survey Monkey, Twitter or your Facebook page.

You can ask your email list. You can visit forums, Yahoo Answers, Ask.com to see what people are asking and want to know about.

Also consider your target market's pain points. What problems are they faced with?

What challenges or issues are most pressing that you think your experts might be able to solve.

Do your homework. You want to make sure to ask good questions.

However, really listen on the call for ways to go deeper or to probe further. This makes for a good interview.

You don't want your book to be surface talk or superficial you want to go deeper.

Make sure to confirm the interview ahead of time as everyone is busy. Also be sure to send a Physical Thank You card thanking the interviewee for allowing you to interview them.

Chapter 10

Make a list of 10 to 12 questions and have someone interview you.

If you want someone to interview you, then you can write out your questions you want to be asked based on Chapter titles and subheadings.

During the interview, you can really provide good content when answering the questions.

You can really go deep when answering the question. After you are done with the interview, you can then write the Introduction and the Conclusion.

Then have it transcribed. I like freeconference.com for recording and you will receive an mp3 to upload to Rev.com who will then transcribe for you. This is super easy and quick.

Chapter 11

Outsource the writing of your book

You can do it one of two ways.

1. You can outsource 10 - 1,000 word articles. 10 different people could potentially write 10 articles based on the topic you give them.

2. You can outsource the whole book to one person.

If you choose this option, be careful, that you are clear on what you want. You should have a list of questions you want answered or topics you want covered.

The downside to this option is the investment it will cost for you to pay someone to write it. Also there is the time issue as you will have to find someone and then give them time to write.

You can check out www.iwriter.com, www.guru.com, www.upwork.com and www.freelancer.com for information on these services.

Be clear on your expectations.
The cost to get someone to write a decent eBook is around $300-$800. The time frame for someone to write it is about 10 to 14 days. It could take longer

If you can afford it, you can have someone write one eBook a month. At the end of the year, you could have 12 books, with very little effort from you.

If you can afford it, you could have two eBooks written a month for a total of 24 at the end of the year with little to no work from you.

You could also keep putting the money you are making at this point from your eBook sales back into writing more eBooks.

If you do this-let's say you went the 1 book a month route every 3 months, you could have an extra book written.

And at the end of the year you could have approximately 15-16 books written by the end of the year.

If you go to the 2 books a month you can potentially have 32 books written by the end of the year.

If you don't want to or you hate to write, then this maybe a great option for you.

You also could write your first 6 books and after that have someone write the rest of them for you. The choice is yours. There are advantages and disadvantages to both.

Outsourcing the article Writing

Advantages

- Means you have to be a super clear (You don't want to leave a freelancer guessing)
- Frees you up to work on other things

- The chances of it being completed are high (If you need some momentum or you've been putting this off for a while, this might be a great option)
- You may get an Experienced writer who will produce great content.

Disadvantages

- Quality could be bad (Remember you pay for what you get)
- The writing won't be your style or voice
- Writer could be inexperienced on topic

I like to run anything written for me by a freelancer thru copyscape.com to make sure they didn't plagiarize. It's easy to use. The cost is minimal about 5 cents per search. For example, I can do 100 searches for $5. You just copy and paste in the spot provided what they provided. I learn this one the hard way.

Years ago, I hired someone to write an eBook for me for a decent price. It took a little longer for him to write it. When I received it, it seemed fine. I took him as his word that he was an ethical writer and a professional.

A couple of months later, I was researching my topic and low and behold the book I paid this freelancer to write copied the whole book almost word for word from another book. It was a nightmare.

Just think, if I hadn't done any research, I may have never known what he had done. Don't let this happen to you.

Write the articles yourself

Advantages

- You can say what you want to say
- You can express your ideas
- It's free
- You can record it in one day
- You will save money
- It's your voice which is what your customers or target market are used to

Disadvantages

- You might procrastinate
- Takes time
- Failed in the past
- Distracted may not be focused
- Need a Strong Why

Wordbotic

You can use Wordbotic

You can use Wordbotic. It is a fill in the blank template. Once it is complete you will need to read and reread it and edit it.

This is software. It is okay to get you started if that is your problem. You will want to go back and add some meat to it.

For more information on this go to www.wordbotic.com.

What to expect

1. 57-Phrased questionnaire to fill out before content is generated
2. Get up to 10k words (at one time) in Microsoft Word at the end of the questionnaire
3. Get up to 500k words. You can use this over several eBooks.

Full Disclaimer: I have used this product. I don't endorse it. I present it here as an option. It was cumbersome for me. If you want some filler sentences it may help.

If you decide to purchase it, watch the tutorials provided.

Chapter 12

A few more things to remember

1. Write down any ideas you might have during the night, while in the shower, doing household chores, while driving, while at work etc., If you don't write them down, you will forget them.

2. Don't get caught up in whether what you are writing will help someone. It will. Just keep writing and move on to the next book. Do your best. With each book you will get better and better and you will get clearer and clearer.

3. Niche down. Don't try to cover everything in one book. That is what a series is for. Think about your topic. Can you break it down any further so you can go deeper?

4. Stay committed. So what if you miss a day. Start writing again the next day. Don't get discouraged. People are writing and publishing books on Amazon Kindle every day. Why not you? They are not smarter than you. They have the same 24 hours as you do. They have families, jobs and distractions just like you but they find the time and so can you.

5. If you get stuck on something or get writer's block, ask yourself what else does my target market want to know. What should they know? Ask yourself what, why, how, when. And keep writing. Still stuck read for a few minutes and then get back to writing.

6. You need to write a lot, write often. Good writers take time to write. Make writing fun by writing about something you are passionate about.

Edit

"Writing is like making love. You have to practice to be good at it." - Morris West, author, the Clowns of God

"I rewrote the ending of Farewell to Arms 39 times before I was satisfied."-Ernest Hemingway

Spend time editing your work. Read over it at least once and make changes as needed. The next time read over it and listen to how it sounds. You will find that some paragraphs don't flow. Some will be too long. Others won't fit. After reading over it a minimum of twice, let it sit a day and two and come back to it and reread it a final time. Ask a friend if they would read it and give you feedback. The next thing you want to do is to find a content editor to review it for you. You can find someone by Googling Content Editor, on Upwork or Guru. Be sure you are clear about what you want as there are several types of editors.

Chapter 14

Marketing Your Book

Book Description

What is your book about? What will your reader learn? What transformation can they expect? How will their life be different? People buy outcomes, transformation.

Book Promotion

Book Promotion starts way before a book is done. Be sure you have a Book Marketing Plan. There are a ton of Book Promotion Group on Facebook. You can tweet your book and do a Facebook post directly from Amazon. To the right of the book below price/add to the cart you will see it.

Book Promotion efforts might include recording a book trailer on your book and why you wrote it. You can record snippets of your book on YouTube. You can also take snippets and put into an article or blog posts. The more you can come up with the better.

Amazon Author Central

Be sure to complete your profile on Amazon Author Central. Add your blog, Twitter and Facebook as well.

Author website

As for your Author Website include the following: Book sales Page, Blog, free offer (squeeze page), About Us, Contact Us, Other Products and Services. If you speak you need a speaker page.

As part of promotion-add any really good reviews to the front, inside cover and back cover of your book.

Blog about your book.

Do videos about your book.

Book Budget-Every book needs a book budget. You need money for Marketing, Book Cover Design, Editing etc.

Book Review

Let's face it Book Reviews sell books. We all need book reviews-a lot of them. Before your book is done try to come up with a list of at least 100 influential people in your niche and then 100 people in your community-include Media-Newspaper, Radio, Local Magazine and Television Personalities. Write a Press Release to them. Keep a spreadsheet to track who you contact and their response. Don't be afraid to follow up. As for influencers, I would send them a free book. You should also be working on building a tribe/community.

Conclusion

Writing is therapeutic. Keep a Journal-reflect on the day

Could you write an eBook if your life depended on it? Well it does.

Your life is depending on you to get better, to make your life better, to make more money, to build a platform, to become an expert.

Your life is depending on you to change what you are currently doing so your life can be the best it can be.

Are you ready for a change?

This book you are going to write is going to change your life, your family's life and your reader's life.

You owe it to everyone to write this amazing book I know you are capable of. Start today.

Success breeds Success.

After you get the 1st eBook done, then just keep writing until the 2nd and the 3^{rd}book are done. You will get better and better and your results will get better and better.

The key is to finish the 1st one and then on to the next one.

Do it now. And one day, you will wake up a published author.

On writing—a matter of exercise. If you work out with weights for fifteen minutes a day over the course of ten years, you're gonna get muscles. If you write for an hour and a half a day for ten years, you're gonna turn into a good writer.- Stephen King

Day 1 Complete You at a Glance Worksheet & Outline

Day 2-8 Write 1,200 words each day for a total of 9,600

Day 9 Edit-read over twice and correct.

Ask a friend to read over it

Day 10 Hire an editor to edit. Write Author Bio. Work on your Book Promotion efforts. Write Book Description.

Quick Start Sheet Audio

Day 1 Complete You at a Glance Worksheet

Day 2 Outline

Day 3 Record yourself talking into your phone using www.freeconferencecall.com.

Day 4 Send to www.rev.com or www.fiverr.com for transcription. Write Book Description. Work on your Book Promotion efforts.

Day 5 Receive copy back from www.rev.com. Write Author Bio. Work on your Book Promotion efforts.

Day 6 & 7 Edit copy for errors

Day 8 & 9 Edit copy for more errors

Day 10 Edit Copy

Quick Start Sheet Outsource

Day 1 Complete You at a Glance Worksheet.

Day 2 Outline.

Day 3 Research www.iwriter.com or www.Upwork.com. Write description of what you want the writer to write.

Day 4 Outsource

Day 5 Write Book Description. Work on your Book Promotion efforts

Day 6 Write Author Bio. Work on your Book Promotion efforts

Day 7 Write 20-500 word articles on your book's topic.

Day 8 Finish writing articles.

Day 9 Record 20 videos to YouTube. The more you can record on your niche or topic the better.

Day 10 Post videos and articles.

Quick Start Sheet Interview (You as the Interviewer)

Day 1 Complete You at a Glance Worksheet & Outline

Day 2 Come up with 12-15 questions to ask the person you are going to Interview

Day 3 Send email to 25 people you might want to interview

Day 4 Schedule interview as soon as possible.

Day 5 Have www.rev.com transcribe.

Day 6 Receive transcript back. Edit. You can do a light edit. If you do a light edit, be sure to let readers know this is a transcript from an interview.

Day 7 Write Book Description. Work on your Book Promotion efforts.

Day 8 Write Author Bio. Work on your Book Promotion efforts.

Day 9 Write 20-500 word articles on your book's topic.

Day 10 Record 20 videos to YouTube. The more you can record on your niche or topic the better. Post videos and articles.

Quick Start Sheet Interview (You as the Interviewee)

Day 1 Complete You at a Glance Worksheet & Outline

Day 2 Come up with 12-15 questions to that you want to be asked.

Day 3 Send email to 5 people you might want to interview you. If you can't get anyone. Ask a friend to interview you and record it.

Day 4 Schedule interview as soon as possible.

Day 5 Have www.rev.com transcribe.

Day 6 Receive transcript back. Edit. You can do a light edit. If you do a light edit, be sure to let readers know this is a transcript from an interview.

Day 7 Write Book Description. Work on your Book Promotion efforts

Day 8 Write Author Bio. Work on your Book Promotion efforts

Day 9 Write 20-500 word articles on your book's topic.

Day 10 Record 20 videos to YouTube. The more you can record on your niche or topic the better. Post videos and articles.

I need your help. When you go to the next page, Kindle gives you an opportunity to share your thoughts and opinions through your Facebook and Twitter account. If you believe your friends and family will benefit from this book, please share your thoughts with them. You might change someone's life, and I would be eternally grateful to you.

If you feel strongly about the contributions this book made to your life, please take a few seconds to post a 5-star review on Amazon. Very few people ever leave 5-star review. So it is a big deal if you do. Writing a 5-

star review is like tipping me $25. I really appreciate the gesture. I feel like a million bucks whenever I get a glowing review.

If you have any questions, you can reach me via Shondamiles@yahoo.com. I will try to respond to your questions as soon as possible. You can also connect with me on Facebook and Twitter.

For more information on Shonda Miles, go to www.shondamiles.com. Shonda Miles offers a range of Products and Services including Multiple Streams of Income-how to make money while you sleep and How to make an extra $100,000 this year.

Other books by Author

10 Ways to Write an Ebook every 10 days

101 Success Questions

Remote Medical Coding Jobs

Tips for Staring an Online Business

How to Love Your Spouse again

How to Double Your Income in 12 Months or less

50 Tips to Jumpstart Your Success

50 Streams of Income

How to Get the Job You Want

21 Ways to Start a Marriage off Right

21 Ways to Break into Coding

21 Ways to make a Blended Family Work

About the Author

Shonda Miles has been self-employed for 18 years. She has owned businesses ranging from an online retail store to a Training Company.

Shonda Miles is the CEO of Shonda Miles International, a company helping organizations and individuals improve performance and achieve their goals. Shonda Miles is here to help you achieve your full potential. Her purpose is to help millions of people achieve their goals and live their God given talent.

Shonda Miles is an Author, Entrepreneur, Speaker, Personal Development Trainer, Business Consultant and Business Coach. She loves reading Nonfiction books, writing business books and shopping. Personal Development is her mission. Shonda speaks, blogs and writes about a variety of personal development topics such as Time Management, Success, Goal Setting and having a Positive Attitude.

Shonda's goal is to help others achieve the level of success they desire.

Shonda Miles is a MBA Graduate. She has several successful businesses.

Shonda Miles can be reached at info@shondamiles.com or via her website at www.shondamiles.com.